Let's Learn About Story Elements: Setting

Let's Learn About Story Elements: Setting
15 Creative Projects That Help Kids Become Better Readers and Writers

Michelle O'Brien-Palmer

illustrations by
Heidi Stephens

Credits

Cover Design: Jaime Lucero

Student Cover Art: Setting Map: Jenny Shroder & Meagan Link
Setting Triorama: Daryl Hutson & Alyson Evans
Sculpted Diorama: Katie Fade

Content Editors: Martha Ivy, teacher, Redmond, WA
Martha Ivy's 4th-grade students, Christa McAuliffe Elementary
Nancy Johnston, teacher, Woodinville, WA
Nancy Johnston's 6th-grade students, Wilder Elementary
Valerie Marshall, teacher, Redmond, WA
Valerie Marshall's 4th-grade students, Christa McAuliffe Elementary
Pam Schild, teacher, Woodinville, WA
Pam Schild's 6th-grade students, Wilder Elementary
Nancie Schonhard, teacher, Woodinville, WA
Nancie Schonhard's 6th-grade students, Wilder Elementary
Joyce Standing, teacher, Redmond, WA
Joyce Standing's students, The Overlake School

Other Contributors: Stephanie Garcia, 6th-grade student, Wilder Elementary
Ann Lyman, teacher, Westhill Elementary
Julee Neupert, teacher, Ben Rush Elementary
Eileen Shaner, teacher, Franconia Elementary
Alesha Thomas, 6th-grade student, Wilder Elementary

Young Authors:

Eunice Chung	Edward Lobdell
Carey DeAngelis	Tara O'Brien
Emily Gibbons	Nick Palmer
Meghan Gibbons	Brian Schnierer
Billy Harris	Michael Strong
Chris Hartsell	Steven Yoo
	Terry Yoo

ISBN 0-590-10715-1

Acknowledgments

I would like to thank the following people for their support and contributions in the creation of *Let's Learn About Story Elements: Setting*.

I am especially grateful to the 6th-grade editors for your honest feedback, project recommendations and inspiration for this book. In our seven months together, you made significant contributions in molding *Let's Learn About Story Elements: Setting* into its final form. I am very proud to have had the opportunity to work through the writing process with you as my editors.

- Thanks to the student editors from Nancy Johnston's class at Wilder Elementary School. Your project ideas and examples were wonderful. I really appreciate your sharing them with the readers of this book.
- Thanks to the student editors from Pam Schild's class at Wilder Elementary School. Your responsible attitude and great ideas really made a difference in this book.
- Thanks to the student editors from Nancie Schonhard's class at Wilder Elementary School. Your suggestions for materials, material lists, and organizing forms will help the readers of this book immensely.

I also extend sincere thanks to those who helped in the production of this book:

To the young authors for their project examples – Kadi Anderson, Eunice Chung, Tierney Creech, Carey DeAngelis, Colby Emerson, Emily Gibbons, Hannah Gibbons, Meghan Gibbons, Lisa Hails, Billy Harris, Jenny Jones, Janet Kim, Kristina Lin, Justin Lobdell, Edward Lobdell, Greg Lundwall, Matt Marcoe, Andy Meade, Willie Neslon, Tara O'Brien, Sean O'Connor, Nick Palmer, Brian Schnierer, Broderick Smith, Sandy Stonesifer, Michael Strong, Terry Yoo, Steven Yoo, Christi Warren, Jamie Weaver, and Jackie White. To Stephanie Garcia and Alesha Thomas for their great project ideas.

To Valerie Marshall and Martha Ivy's students at McAuliffe Elementary – thank you for inviting me into your classroom. I had such fun talking with you and sharing the process of writing this book. I really appreciate the special effort you made to help me problem solve.

To Joyce Standing's students at The Overlake School – you are so enthusiastic and excited about reading and writing it was inspiring to be among you. Thank you for sharing your projects.

To Martha Ivy, Ann Lyman, Nancy Johnston, Valerie Marshall, Julee Neupert, Eileen Shaner, Pam Schild, Nancie Schonhard, and Joyce Standing for sharing your project ideas.

To Heidi Stephens for your wonderfully inspired illustrations.

To Evelyn Sansky for your love and friendship. To Bob and Marcene Christoverson for your wisdom and guidance, to my son, Nick Palmer for your hugs and patience, and to my husband, Gid Palmer for your constant love and support.

Setting Projects

is **dedicated** to every child involved in this book

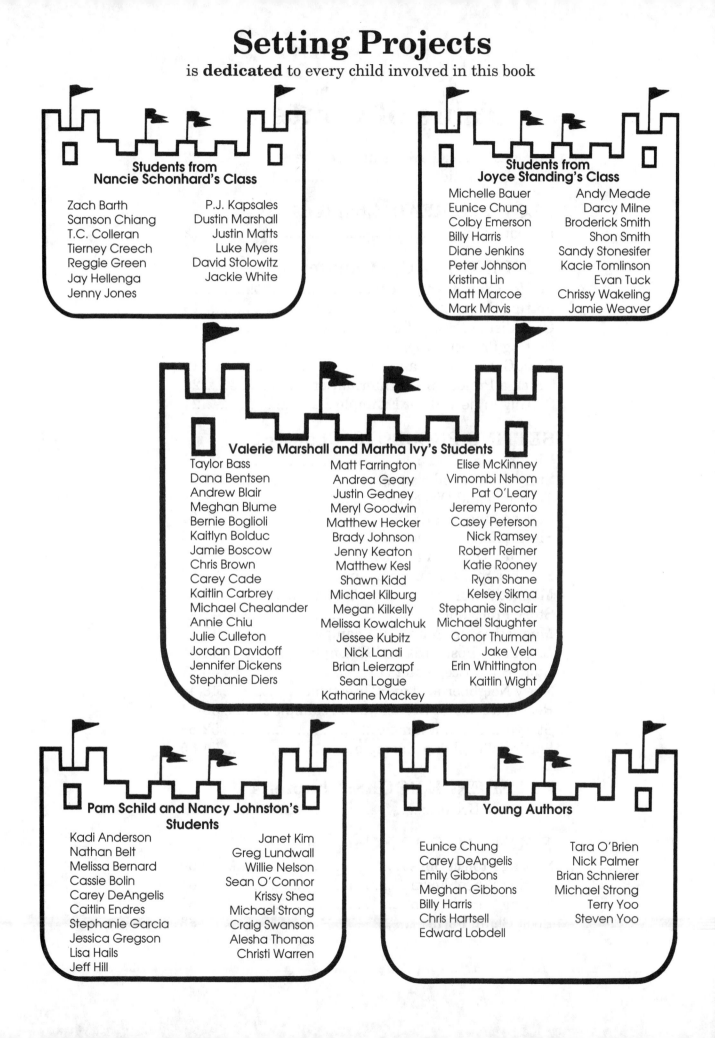

Students from Nancie Schonhard's Class

Zach Barth
Samson Chiang
T.C. Colleran
Tierney Creech
Reggie Green
Jay Hellenga
Jenny Jones

P.J. Kapsales
Dustin Marshall
Justin Matts
Luke Myers
David Stolowitz
Jackie White

Students from Joyce Standing's Class

Michelle Bauer
Eunice Chung
Colby Emerson
Billy Harris
Diane Jenkins
Peter Johnson
Kristina Lin
Matt Marcoe
Mark Mavis

Andy Meade
Darcy Milne
Broderick Smith
Shon Smith
Sandy Stonesifer
Kacie Tomlinson
Evan Tuck
Chrissy Wakeling
Jamie Weaver

Valerie Marshall and Martha Ivy's Students

Taylor Bass
Dana Bentsen
Andrew Blair
Meghan Blume
Bernie Boglioli
Kaitlyn Bolduc
Jamie Boscow
Chris Brown
Carey Cade
Kaitlin Carbrey
Michael Chealander
Annie Chiu
Julie Culleton
Jordan Davidoff
Jennifer Dickens
Stephanie Diers

Matt Farrington
Andrea Geary
Justin Gedney
Meryl Goodwin
Matthew Hecker
Brady Johnson
Jenny Keaton
Matthew Kesl
Shawn Kidd
Michael Kilburg
Megan Kilkelly
Melissa Kowalchuk
Jessee Kubitz
Nick Landi
Brian Leierzapf
Sean Logue
Katharine Mackey

Elise McKinney
Vimombi Nshom
Pat O'Leary
Jeremy Peronto
Casey Peterson
Nick Ramsey
Robert Reimer
Katie Rooney
Ryan Shane
Kelsey Sikma
Stephanie Sinclair
Michael Slaughter
Conor Thurman
Jake Vela
Erin Whittington
Kaitlin Wight

Pam Schild and Nancy Johnston's Students

Kadi Anderson
Nathan Belt
Melissa Bernard
Cassie Bolin
Carey DeAngelis
Caitlin Endres
Stephanie Garcia
Jessica Gregson
Lisa Hails
Jeff Hill

Janet Kim
Greg Lundwall
Willie Nelson
Sean O'Connor
Krissy Shea
Michael Strong
Craig Swanson
Alesha Thomas
Christi Warren

Young Authors

Eunice Chung
Carey DeAngelis
Emily Gibbons
Meghan Gibbons
Billy Harris
Chris Hartsell
Edward Lobdell

Tara O'Brien
Nick Palmer
Brian Schnierer
Michael Strong
Terry Yoo
Steven Yoo

Table of Contents

Introduction
for Parents and Teachers

Let's Learn About Story Elements: Setting was written to give children (2nd-5th grade) an enticing selection of reading extension projects focused on story setting. Each project was chosen by other kids as one they would especially recommend. This text is part of the Let's Learn About Story Elements series, which includes books on plot and character.

Although the text speaks to children directly, it will require adult supervision and guidance in most cases. There are projects which require an Exacto™ knife, scissors and sometimes other potentially dangerous appliances. Each chapter includes front pages with a visual representation of chapter contents. This is to help kids visually identify those experiences which are of interest to them. Whenever extra information might be helpful to parents or teachers it will be found in italics just under the project head. The second chapter (Keeping Track) includes organizing forms for books, projects and materials. There is also a chapter of forms for you to use in your classroom. Make as many copies as you need of these forms as well as any blank forms you find in other chapters. The resource list in Chapter 4 is intended to provide a number of excellent references for bringing literature into your home or classroom.

Each project idea in this book is meant to be taken as liberally as possible. There is no one right way to do any of them. The more variations created, the more exciting the process will be.

Foreword to Kids

I love to read! The kids who helped me write this book love reading too. We decided to create three books which celebrate reading and share some of our favorite reading projects with you. We worked together for seven months in a school library which looks much like the illustration on page 5; we shared project ideas, tested those ideas, and finally came up with our list of favorite projects related to story setting. We hope you enjoy these projects as much as we do.

The chapter called Keeping Track was designed to help you organize your project materials and keep track of the books you read and the projects you complete. You can copy these forms and use them to gather your project supplies.

Some projects will be new to you and some may be similar to projects you've made before. Use your imagination to create your own unique projects.

Have fun celebrating your favorite books!

I Love to Read

Chapter 1

Introduction

This chapter provides a brief introduction to each main chapter. *Let's Learn About Story Elements: Setting* was written with the help of over 100 kids. They were part of the writing and editing process. The young authors who share their unedited project examples in the book are listed below:

Eunice Chung	Edward Lobdell
Carey DeAngelis	Tara O'Brien
Emily Gibbons	Nick Palmer
Meghan Gibbons	Brian Schnierer
Billy Harris	Michael Strong
Chris Hartsell	Steven Yoo
	Terry Yoo

Chapter 2: Keeping Track

This chapter is set up to help readers organize and track their books, projects, and project materials. The Book Chain helps more experienced readers set reading goals and track their progress. The Track-a-Project Sheet gives readers instant feedback as to the types of projects they have created. The Checklist of Project Decorating Items and the Setting Project Supply Sheet are great tools for setting up an area with materials you'll need to create the projects in this book.

Chapter 3: Setting Projects

Setting is not always an easy concept for younger children to grasp. The setting projects in this book are intended to help make this concept more concrete. This chapter's projects range in complexity from simple Story Stones to the creation of a Story Neighborhood made of milk cartons, boxes and other recycled items. Readers can travel through the story setting on a Magnetic Story Map they draw themselves. Using Dioramas, a Triorama or a Shoebox Story Scene, readers can create a scene right out of the story. Story Props, Story Snow Scenes, and Storyboards become lively additions to any book-talk, book report or story retelling.

Chapter 4: This chapter provides a number of excellent references for bringing literature into your home or classroom.

Chapter 5: Forms

The forms in this chapter accompany the projects in the book. They are meant to be copied for classroom use.

Keeping Track

Chapter 2

To Help You Keep Track...

Project Organizers

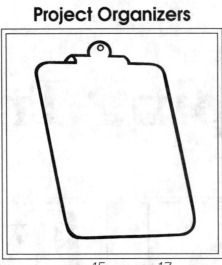

page 15 – page 17

Book Chain

page 18 – page 19

Track-a-Project Sheet

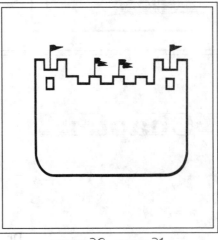

page 20- page 21

I LOVE TO READ

Setting Project List

Name:_____

Date: _____

Select one of the following book projects to share with your class:

- ❑ Story Stones
- ❑ Triorama
- ❑ Setting Map
- ❑ Simple Diorama
- ❑ Sculpted Diorama
- ❑ Shoebox Story Scene
- ❑ Magnetic Story Frame
- ❑ Story Props
- ❑ Magnetic Story Map
- ❑ Literature Postcards
- ❑ Story Snow Scene
- ❑ Story Neighborhood
- ❑ Reader's Theater Scenery
- ❑ Storyboard
- ❑ Setting Wheel

Checklist of Project Decorating Items

- ❏ aluminum foil
- ❏ beads
- ❏ beans
- ❏ bottle caps
- ❏ brass fasteners
- ❏ buttons
- ❏ cans
- ❏ cardboard
- ❏ cardboard tubes
- ❏ clay
- ❏ colored moss
- ❏ colored paper
- ❏ colored pencils
- ❏ colored plastic wrap
- ❏ computer paper
- ❏ construction paper
- ❏ cookie cutters
- ❏ cotton balls (colored)
- ❏ cotton swabs
- ❏ crepe paper
- ❏ drinking straws
- ❏ egg cartons
- ❏ fabric paint
- ❏ fabric scraps
- ❏ feathers
- ❏ felt squares
- ❏ film containers
- ❏ finger paints
- ❏ glitter
- ❏ glue stick
- ❏ googly eyes
- ❏ hangers
- ❏ lace
- ❏ magazines
- ❏ margarine tubs

- ❏ markers
- ❏ milk cartons
- ❏ newspapers
- ❏ plain paper
- ❏ paper clips
- ❏ paper cups
- ❏ paper plates
- ❏ paper scraps
- ❏ pastels
- ❏ pie tins
- ❏ pipe cleaners
- ❏ popsicle sticks
- ❏ ribbon
- ❏ sand
- ❏ shells
- ❏ spices
- ❏ sponges
- ❏ spools
- ❏ stickers
- ❏ string
- ❏ tagboard pieces
- ❏ tissue paper
- ❏ toothpicks
- ❏ twigs
- ❏ wallpaper pieces
- ❏ wire
- ❏ wood scraps
- ❏ wrapping paper
- ❏ yarn
- ❏ _____
- ❏ _____
- ❏ _____
- ❏ _____
- ❏ _____
- ❏ _____

Setting Project Supplies

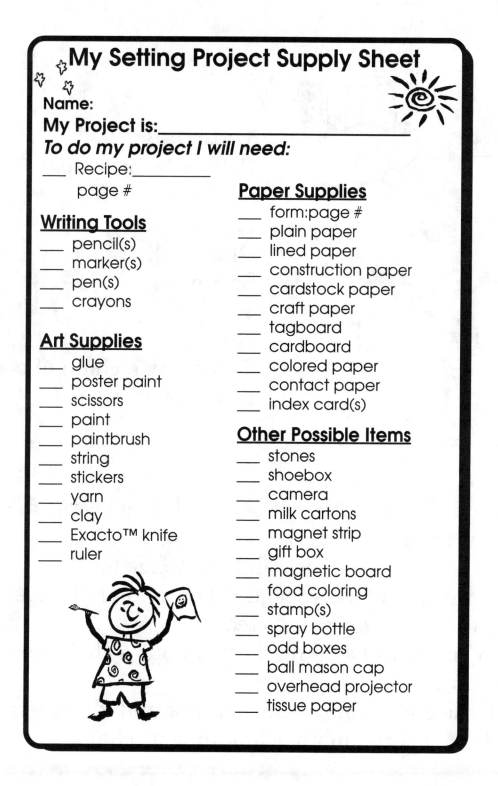

My Setting Project Supply Sheet

Name:

My Project is:_____

To do my project I will need:

___ Recipe:_____

    page #

Writing Tools

___ pencil(s)

___ marker(s)

___ pen(s)

___ crayons

Art Supplies

___ glue

___ poster paint

___ scissors

___ paint

___ paintbrush

___ string

___ stickers

___ yarn

___ clay

___ Exacto™ knife

___ ruler

Paper Supplies

___ form:page #

___ plain paper

___ lined paper

___ construction paper

___ cardstock paper

___ craft paper

___ tagboard

___ cardboard

___ colored paper

___ contact paper

___ index card(s)

Other Possible Items

___ stones

___ shoebox

___ camera

___ milk cartons

___ magnet strip

___ gift box

___ magnetic board

___ food coloring

___ stamp(s)

___ spray bottle

___ odd boxes

___ ball mason cap

___ overhead projector

___ tissue paper

Book Chain

The book chain idea came from 6th-graders Alesha Thomas and Stefanie Garcia. They suggest hanging the chains in your room or using them for decorations at holidays.

Materials:
Colored/white paper
Markers/pencil
Page 63
Glue stick
Scissors

Goal:
To display a chain of book titles you've read.

Steps:

1. Determine the number of book titles you want to include on your chain.
2. Copy the goal form and fill it out (page 63).
3. Copy the chain forms (page 63) onto colored paper.
4. Read the book you've selected.
5. When you've finished reading, fill out a chain form and cut it out.
6. Hook the ends around the last link and glue them together to form another link in your chain.

Book Chain Examples

Book Chain Goal Sheet

Today's Date: *10/11*

Name: *Nick Palmer*

Number of books I want to read and include in my chain

_____*10*_____.

Starting date _____*10/12*_____   Goal ending date *6/12*_____

Types of books (genres) I want to include:

☑ Adventure   ☑ Humor   ☐ Realistic Fiction
☑ Biography   ☐ Historical Fiction ☐ Other:_____
☑ Courage   ☑ Mystery
   and Survival   ☐ Poetry
☐ Fairytale   ☑ Science Fiction

Title: *Hatchet*

Author: *Gary Paulson*

Title: *River*

Author: *Gary Paulson*

Title: *The Old Man and the Sea*

Author: *E. Hemmingway*

Title: _____

Author: _____

Title: _____

Author: _____

Track-a-Project Sheet

This sheet helps kids monitor and evaluate the projects they have completed. For fast tracking, kids recommend color coding each type of project.

Materials:
Page 60
Scissors
Pencil/pen
O-Ring
Hole punch
Laminating materials

Goal:
To keep track of the projects you've created.

Steps:
1. Copy the form on page 60 onto colored paper.
2. Cut out the form and write the project and book title inside.
3. Did you enjoy making this project? Check the box that fits your answer. Then laminate the project sheet.
4. Punch a hole in the circle at the bottom of the sheet. Place the sheet on an O-ring.
5. Share your favorite projects with friends and be sure to tell them why you enjoyed the project so much.

Setting Project Sheet Example

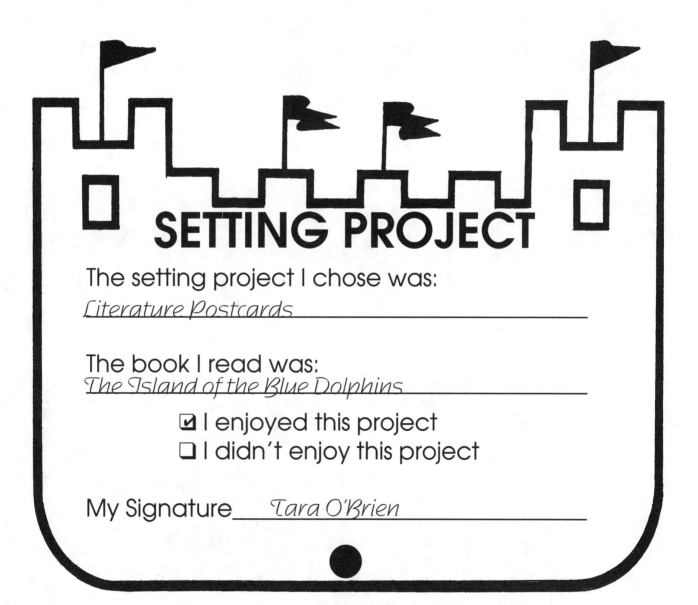

SETTING PROJECT

The setting project I chose was:

Literature Postcards

The book I read was:
The Island of the Blue Dolphins

☑ I enjoyed this project
☐ I didn't enjoy this project

My Signature _Tara O'Brien_

Setting Projects

Chapter 3

Chapter Contents

The Setting tells us when and where, so we can feel as if we were really there.

The author paints a picture for you and me. Use your imagination and the setting you'll see!

Story Stones

page 26

Triorama

page 28

Setting Map

page 30

Simple Diorama

page 32

Sculpted Diorama

My Diorama for **Tuck Everlasting**

page 34

Shoebox Story Scene

page 36

24

Chapter Contents

Magnetic Story Frame

Story Props

Magnetic Story Map

Literature Postcards

Story Snow Scene

Story Neighborhood

Reader's Theater Scenery

Storyboard

Setting Wheel

Story Stones

Story Stones can feature story characters or story scenes. Kids enjoy trading stones from their story collections.

Materials:
Smooth stones
Glue
Poster paints/markers
Paintbrush
Construction paper
Pencil
Yarn/fabric scraps

Goal:
To decorate a stone with the image of a story character or story scene.

Steps:
1. Find four smooth stones from outside. Wash and dry each one.
2. Decide which characters and scenes you want to draw on your stones.
3. Draw your design on each stone in pencil.
4. Use paint or markers to fill in your design and paste on any extra items such as yarn or fabric scraps.
5. Share your Story Stones with friends.

Story Stone Examples

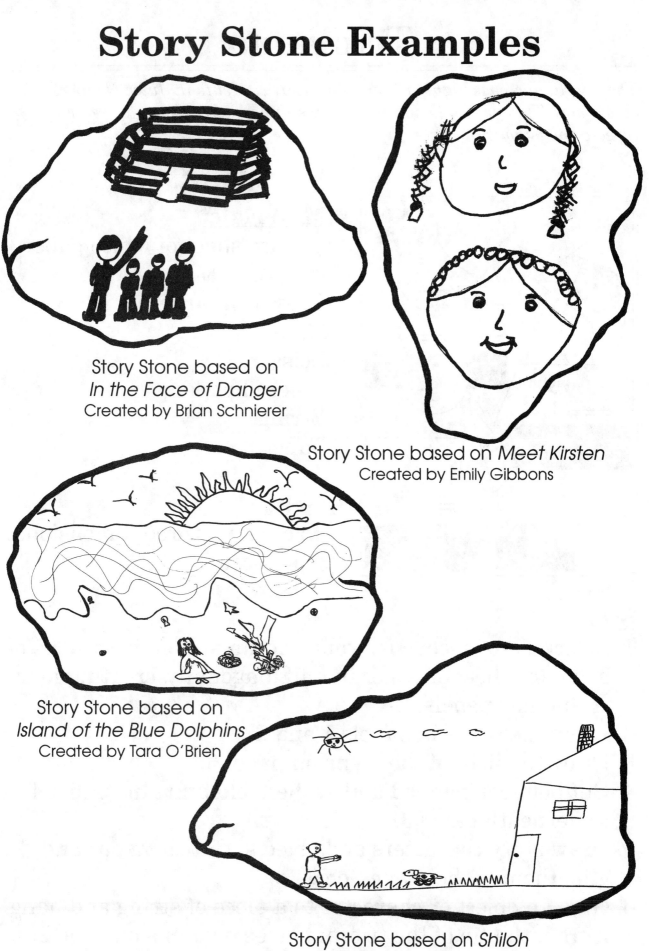

Story Stone based on
In the Face of Danger
Created by Brian Schnierer

Story Stone based on *Meet Kirsten*
Created by Emily Gibbons

Story Stone based on
Island of the Blue Dolphins
Created by Tara O'Brien

Story Stone based on *Shiloh*
Created by Terry Yoo

Triorama

The triorama comes highly recommended by students in Julee Neupert's classroom. This project is an amazingly simple and fun way to create a three-dimensional story scene.

Materials:

Square sheet of white paper (12-by-12 inches)
Crayons/markers
Glue
Scissors
Colored paper
String
Tape

Goal:

To create a three-dimensional story scene.

Steps:

1. Select a story scene for your triorama. Fold both sides of a square sheet of paper in half diagonally, creating four triangular panels.
2. Draw the scene in panels 1 and 2.
3. Draw the floor of the scene on panel 3.
4. Cut between panel 3 and 4, then fold and glue panel 4 underneath panel 3.
5. Draw story characters and objects. Cut them out and glue them to the scene floor.
6. Glue an object or character to a piece of string and hang it from the tip of the triorama (see example on page 29).

Triorama Directions

Step 1

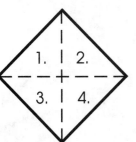

Fold both sides of 12-by-12 inch paper in half diagonally.

Step 2

Draw the scene in panels one and two.

Step 3

Draw the floor of the scene on panel 3.

Step 4

Cut between panel 3 and 4, then fold and glue panel 4 underneath panel 3.

Step 5

Draw characters and story objects. Cut them out and glue them to the scene floor.

Step 6

Glue an object or character to a piece of string and hang it from the tip of the triorama.

Sample

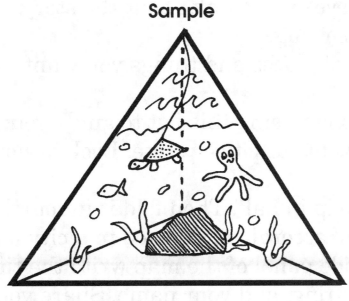

Share your finished triorama.

Setting Map

Ann Lyman's students enjoy drawing maps of how they imagine the main story setting would look. This is a great partner project.

Lake and Forest
Hatchet Map

Materials:
Craft paper (23 1/2-by-18 inches)
Markers/pens

Goal:
To draw a map of a story's main setting.

Steps:

1. Close your eyes and think about the story. Imagine a map of the setting.
2. Write a list of places and things you want to include on your map.
3. Draw your map using this list to guide you.
4. Find a map of your city or state. Look at how it is folded.
5. Fold your map in half. Then fold it in fourths using the same kind of accordion fold used in a city map.
6. On an outside panel of the map write the title of the book, the setting, and your name. Share your map with friends.

Setting Map Example

This setting map was based on *The Cay*

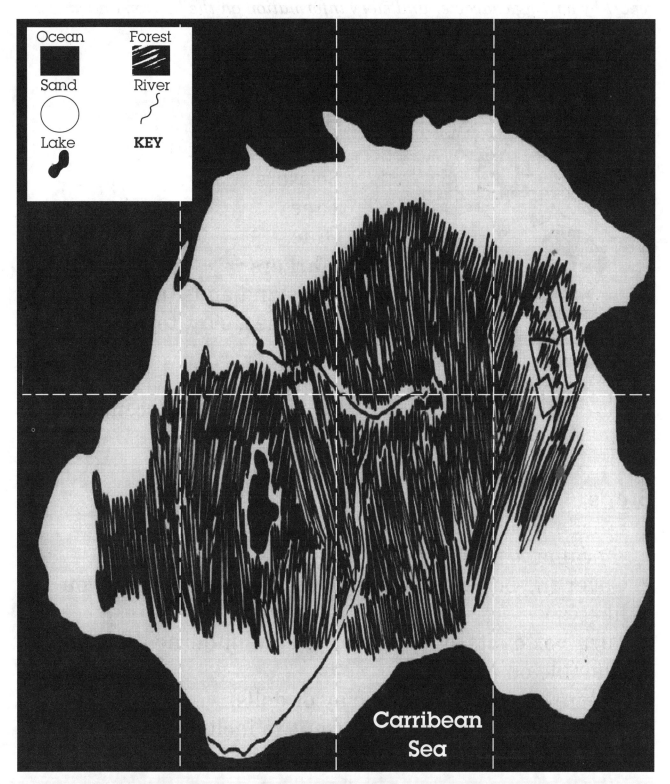

This project was created by Michael Strong and Chris Hartsell

Simple Diorama

This diorama is simple to make. Characters can be created with clay or requisitioned from the toy chest. It could easily be transformed into a book report by writing character and story information on the box top and sides.

Materials:
Gift box
Paper (all sorts)
Scissors
Tape
Glue
Markers
Odds and ends (rocks, branches, clay, toys)

Goal:
To create a story scene in a box.

Steps:
1. Decide which story scene you want to use in your diorama.
2. Cover the box outside and/or inside with paper if you like.
3. Turn box on its side, placing the lid underneath (see example on page 33).
4. Create characters out of clay or dolls.
5. Draw any other items you want to include.
6. Create the scene from odds and ends.

Simple Diorama Example

Simple diorama based on *The Summer of My German Soldier*
Created by Carey DeAngelis

Sculpted Diorama

The Sculpted Diorama is especially fun to create. The sculpted back is like scenery on a stage. Adult supervision may be required for cutting.

Materials:
Shoebox
Paper (all sorts)
Scissors
Tape
Glue
Markers
Odds and ends (rocks, branches, clay)

Goal:
To create a 3-D story scene from a shoebox.

Steps:
1. Decide which story scene you want to use in your diorama.
2. Remove the shoebox lid and turn box on its long side so that the opening is facing you. Cut off the top section of the box.
3 Cut the sides at an angle as shown on page 35.
4. Cut the back of the box to fit the scene.
5. Create a setting scene and characters from odds and ends, clay, or construction paper.
6. Place or glue the items and characters inside the box.

Sculpted Diorama Directions

Steps 1 and 2

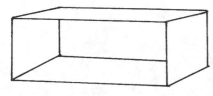

Remove shoe box lid, turn box on its side and cut off the top section.

Step 3

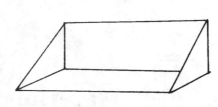

Cut sides at an angle.

Step 4

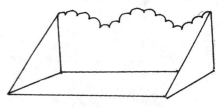

Cut the back of the box to fit the scene.

Steps 5 and 6

Create setting scenes and characters from odds and ends, clay, or construction paper. Place or glue them inside the shoebox.

Sample

Share your sculpted diorama with friends.

Shoebox Story Scene

The students in Pam Schild's class at Wilder Elementary enjoy creating many different reading extension projects. The Shoebox Story Scene was one of their favorite projects. Adult supervision may be required for cutting.

Materials:
Shoebox (with lid)
Markers
Scissors/Exacto™ knife
Pencil/crayons
Construction paper
Glue/tape

Goal:
To create a story scene within a viewing box.

Steps:
1. Decide which story scene you want to create. Cut a piece of construction paper to fit inside the bottom of a shoe box.
2. Create a 3-dimensional scene from the story on the construction paper.
3. Cover the box and lid with paper.
4. Cut a 2-by-2 inch window in the center of one end of the lid. This will let light in as you view your scene.
5. Decorate the box outside.
6. Cut a small peek hole in one end of the box.
7. Place the scene in the bottom of the box.

Shoebox Story Scene Directions

Step 1

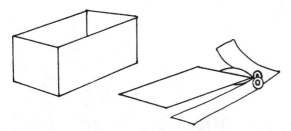

Cut a piece of construction paper to fit inside the bottom of the shoebox.

Step 2

Create a 3-dimensional scene from a story on the construction paper.

Step 3

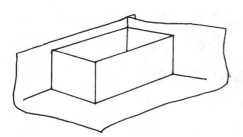

Cover the shoe box and lid with construction paper or shelf paper.

Step 4

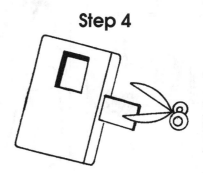

Cut a two inch square window in the center of one end of the lid.

Step 5

Decorate the box with items from the story.

Step 6

Cut a small peek hole in one end of the box.

Step 7

Place the scene in the bottom of the box and share it with your friends.

Magnetic Story Frame

The Magnetic Story Frame is a great recycling project. Ball mason jars are used for storing homemade jams. They can be found in most grocery stores.

Materials:
Tagboard and paper
Scissors and glue
Pencil/markers
Tissue paper
Magnetic strip (3 inch)
Ball mason cap

Goal:
To create a magnetic story scene.

Steps:
1. Use the rim of the cap's metal lid to trace two circles on tagboard and paper. Use the band's rim to trace a larger circle onto tagboard. Cut out the three circles.
2. Draw a story scene on the paper circle and glue it to the smaller tagboard circle.
3. Turn the band over and paste the story scene face down on the inside.
4. Place wadded tissue inside the frame. Paste the larger tagboard circle to the edge of the frame.
5. Stick the magnetic strip to the tagboard.

Story Frame Directions

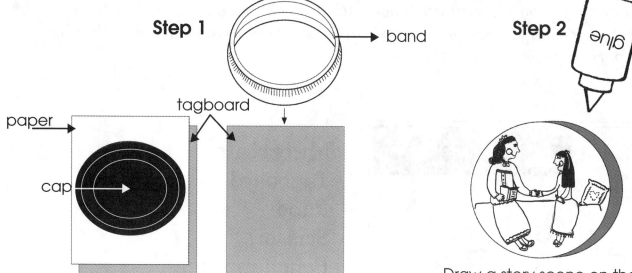

Step 1

band

tagboard

paper

cap

Step 2

glue

Draw a story scene on the paper circle and glue it to the same sized tagboard circle.

Using the rim of the cap's metal lid trace one circle on paper and the other on tagboard. Using the band's rim trace and cut a larger circle on tagboard.

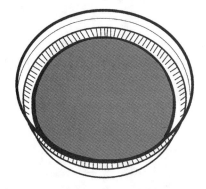

Step 3

Turn the cap band over. Glue the circles face down to the inside of the band.

Step 4

With the frame upside down, place wadded tissue inside the cap. Glue the larger tagboard circle to the outside edge of the cap's band.

Sample
by Meghan Gibbons

Step 5

magnet

Stick the magnetic strip to the tagboard.

Turn your frame over and place it on your refrigerator.

Story Props

Story props complement any book-talk or book presentation. As shown on the next page, story props take many different forms. Imagination is the most important ingredient in this project.

Materials:
Tagboard
Paper
Scissors
Pencil/markers
Glue
Odds and ends
Clay

Goal:
To create a story prop for use in a retelling.

Steps:
1. List items which were very important to the story. Select two or three to use in your retelling.
2. Make the items with clay or other materials and attach them to a large piece of tagboard.
3. Write the book title and your name on the project.
4. Include any other items which will help retell the story.

Story Prop Examples

Metropolitan
Cafe
Sandwich
Grilled cheese sandwich	$1.95
Ham sandwich	$1.95
BLT	$1.95
Club sandwich	$1.95
Grilled chicken sandwich	$1.95

Snacks
Peanutbutter crackers	$ .50
Bubble gum lime, raspberry, grape	$ .25
Cereal	$ .45
Cookies Chocolate chip, oatmeal	$ .50
Chocolate Mousse cake	$2.00

Beverage
Juices	
Pineapple	$ .35
Apple	$ .35
Other	
Coffee	$ .25
Water	

From the Mixed—up Files of
Mrs. Basil E. Frankweiler

By Billy Harris & Eunice Chung

Magnetic Story Map

Valerie Marshall and Martha Ivy created the Setting Map on the right for their classroom magnetic board. The students in their classroom made character magnets and attached them to the map as they followed it through the story.

Materials:
Large sheet of paper
Markers/pencils
Overhead projector
Tape
Magnetic writing board
Character magnets

Goal:
To create a story map for use on a magnetic board.

Steps:
1. Draw a larger version of a map in a book by using an overhead projector.
2. Tape the map to a magnetic writing board.
3. Purchase magnetic figures or make magnets to represent the characters.
4. As you and your classmates read through the story, place your character magnets at the appropriate setting location on the map.

Magnetic Story Map Example

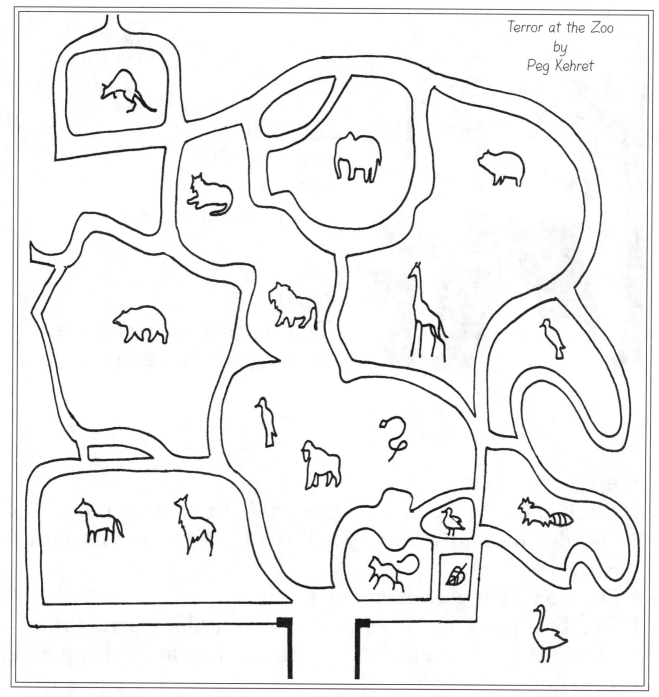

Terror at the Zoo
by
Peg Kehret

This magnetic story map was from Valerie Marshall and Martha Ivy's 4th-grade classroom.

Literature Postcards

Writing a Literature Postcard to a pen pal is a unique way of sharing a reading experience. Kids enjoy corresponding with each other in words and pictures.

Materials:
Index card(s)
Stamp(s)
Pen/pencil/markers

Goal:
To discuss a story you are reading with a pen pal.

Steps:
1. Find a book you and your pen pal both want to read.
2. Decide how many pages you'll read before the first postcard.
3. Decide which person will write first.
4. The first person sends a postcard describing something they really like in the story. You can include writing and drawings.
5. The other person sends a postcard back saying how they like the book.
6. Continue sending postcards until you've finished reading the story.

Literature Postcard Examples

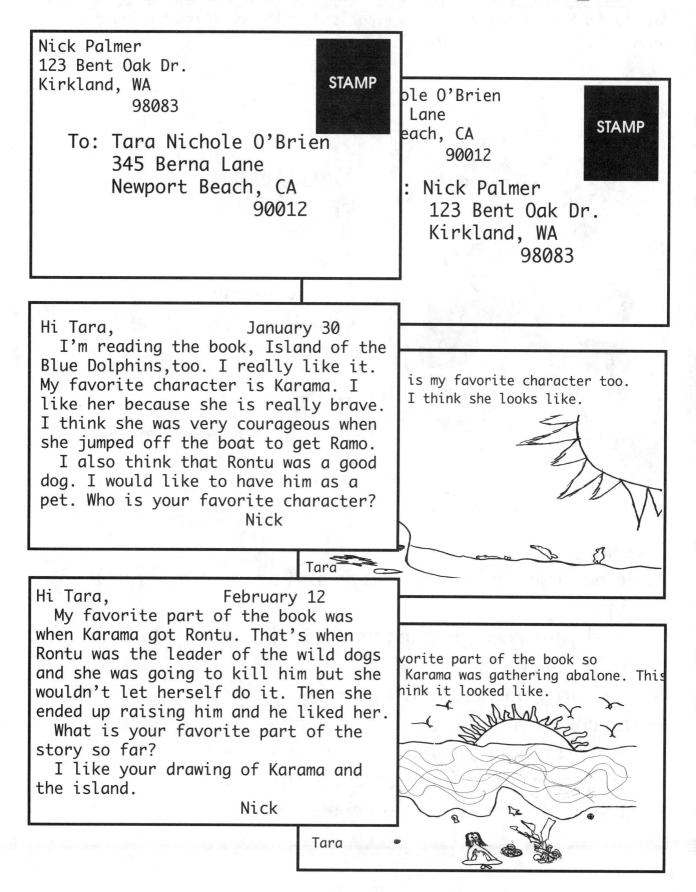

Nick Palmer
123 Bent Oak Dr.
Kirkland, WA
        98083

STAMP

To: Tara Nichole O'Brien
    345 Berna Lane
    Newport Beach, CA
        90012

ole O'Brien
 Lane
each, CA
    90012

STAMP

: Nick Palmer
   123 Bent Oak Dr.
   Kirkland, WA
       98083

Hi Tara,   January 30
   I'm reading the book, Island of the
Blue Dolphins, too. I really like it.
My favorite character is Karama. I
like her because she is really brave.
I think she was very courageous when
she jumped off the boat to get Ramo.
   I also think that Rontu was a good
dog. I would like to have him as a
pet. Who is your favorite character?
                        Nick

is my favorite character too.
I think she looks like.

Tara

Hi Tara,   February 12
   My favorite part of the book was
when Karama got Rontu. That's when
Rontu was the leader of the wild dogs
and she was going to kill him but she
wouldn't let herself do it. Then she
ended up raising him and he liked her.
   What is your favorite part of the
story so far?
   I like your drawing of Karama and
the island.
                        Nick

vorite part of the book so
 Karama was gathering abalone. This
hink it looked like.

Tara

Story Snow Scene

Molding a Story Snow Scene is a great winter project. It is a unique and incredibly fun way to extend a literature experience.

Materials:
Spray bottles
Water
Snow
Food coloring
Camera
Paper/pencil

Goal:
To mold a three-dimensional story snow scene.

Steps:
1. Select a scene from the story and draw it on a piece of paper.
2. Mold your scene in the snow (small houses, snow figures, buildings, etc).
3. Fill spray bottles with water and food coloring to create the colors you want to include in your snow scene.
4. Paint the scenery with the spray bottles.
5. Share your story snow scene with friends.
6. Take a picture of your snow scene before it melts.

Story Snow Scene Directions

Step 1

Select a scene from the story
and draw it on a piece of paper.

Step 2

Mold your scene in the snow (small
houses, snow figures, buildings, etc.)

Step 3

Fill spray bottles with food coloring and water to create the colors you want to
include in your snow scene.

Sample

Paint the scenery with spray bottles and share your story snow
scenes with friends. Don't forget to take a picture!

Story Neighborhood

Building a Story Neighborhood takes story comprehension and imagination. Kids rate this as one of their favortie projects.

Materials:
Milk cartons/boxes
Construction paper
Scissors
Pencil/markers
Glue/tape/paste
Odds and ends

Goal:
To create a story neighborhood out of everyday materials.

Steps:
1. Think about your favorite character's neighborhood in the story.
2. Draw a picture of what the neighborhood might look like. Collect project materials.
3. Cut a sheet of construction paper to fit around each carton and box building.
4. Glue the paper to the cartons and boxes.
5. Create windows, doors and other items out of construction paper. Glue them to the carton and box buildings.
6. Arrange the buildings, trees, etc. to form the story neighborhood.

Story Neighborhood Directions

Steps 1 and 2

Draw a picture of the story neighborhood.

Step 3

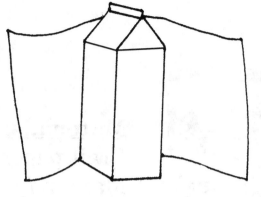

Cut a sheet of construction paper to fit around each carton and box.

Step 4

Glue the paper to the cartons or boxes.

Step 5

Create construction paper windows and doors. Glue them to the buildings.

Step 6

Arrange the buildings, trees, etc. to form the story neighborhood.

Share your story neighborhood with your friends!

Reader's Theater Scenery

The Reader's Theater Scenery is a perfect backdrop for puppet characters, character masks or dressing up as a character in a story dramatization.

Materials:
Craft paper
Markers/pencils
Paint
Paper
Paint brushes

Goal:
To create story scenery for a play.

Steps:
1. Think about where the story takes place and imagine what the setting would look like.
2. Draw a picture of the setting on a piece of paper.
3. Get your materials ready and create your scenery using craft paper and paint supplies. It really works well to outline items in black paint and then fill in the colors. It makes the scenery stand out.
4. Let the scenery dry, and then hang it up to use it in your play.

Reader's Theater Scenery Example

Scenery created by Edward Lobdell for the book, *Silver*

Storyboard

Storyboards are a very graphic tool in a presentation or retelling. Martha Ivy and Valerie Marshall's students draw scenes from stories as they are read aloud. These scenes are then added to their classroom storyboard.

Materials:
Tagboard
Paper
Ruler
Pencil/markers
Glue

Goal:
To create a board that shows six or more scenes in a story.

Steps:
1. List at least six important story events.
2. Think through what happened in the events. Draw a picture of each event.
3. Write a short sentence underneath each drawing explaining the scene.
4. Glue the scenes to a piece of tagboard and share your storyboard with friends.

Storyboard Example

Shiloh Story Board by Terry and Steven Yoo

Shiloh follows Marty home.

Shiloh was returned to its owner.

Shiloh got attacked by a German shepherd.

Shiloh goes to the doctor.

Setting Wheel

Many students make a Guess the Setting version of the Setting Wheel. They don't reveal the book title so that the other students guess which book they read.

Materials:
2 sheets of cardstock
Pages 61 and 62
Markers or colored pens
Scissors
Exacto™ knife
Brass fastener

Goal:
To share four different
  scenes from a story.

Steps:
1. Copy the forms on pages 61 and 62 onto cardstock.
2. Cut out each form.
3. Write the title, author, and your name on the outside of the the form from page 61. Decorate it with story items.
4. Draw a picture of your favorite story scene in the first quadrant of the form on page 62. Draw a scene from the beginning of the story in the second quadrant, the middle of the story in the third quadrant, and the end of the story in the fourth quadrant.
5. Ask an adult to use an Exacto™ knife to make a small **x** in the center of each circle. Insert the brass fastener into this opening.
6. Share your setting wheel with other students.

54

Setting Wheel Directions

Steps 1 and 2

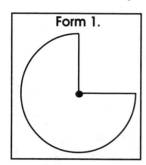
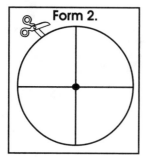

Copy and then cut out the forms found on pages 61 and 62.

Step 3

Write the book title, author's name, and your name on form 1.

Step 4

Using form 2 - draw a picture of your favorite story scene in quadrant 1. Draw a scene from the story beginning in quadrant 2, middle in quadrant 3 and end in quadrant 4.

Step 5

Ask an adult to cut an **x** in the center of both cricles with an Ex-acto™ knife. Insert a brass fastener into the center.

Sample

Share your Setting Wheel with your friends.

Reference Books

Chapter 4

Reference Books

Author	Book Title	Publisher
Brown, Hazel Cambourne, Brian	*Read and Retell*	Heinemann Educational Books, 1990
Calkins, Lucy McCormick	*Lessons from a Child*	Heinemann Educational Books, 1986
Johnson, Terry D. Louis, Daphne R.	*Literacy Through Literature*	Heinemann Educational Books, 1987
Luekens, Rebecca J.	*A Critical Handbook of Children's Literature*	HarperCollins Publishers, 1990
Norton, Donna	*The Impact of Literature-Based Reading*	Macmillan Publishing Company, 1992
O'Brien-Palmer, Michelle	*Beyond Book Reports*	Scholastic Professional Books, 1997
O'Brien-Palmer, Michelle	*Great Graphic Organizers*	Scholastic Professional Books, 1997
O'Brien-Palmer, Michelle	*Let's Learn About Story Elements: Plot*	Scholastic Professional Books, 1998
O'Brien-Palmer, Michelle	*Let's Learn About Story Elements: Character*	Scholastic Professional Books, 1998
Rothlein, Liz Meinbach, Anita Meyer	*The Literature Connection*	Scott, Foresman and Company, 1991
Routman, Reggie	*Invitations*	Heinemann Educational Books, 1991

Forms to Copy

Chapter 5

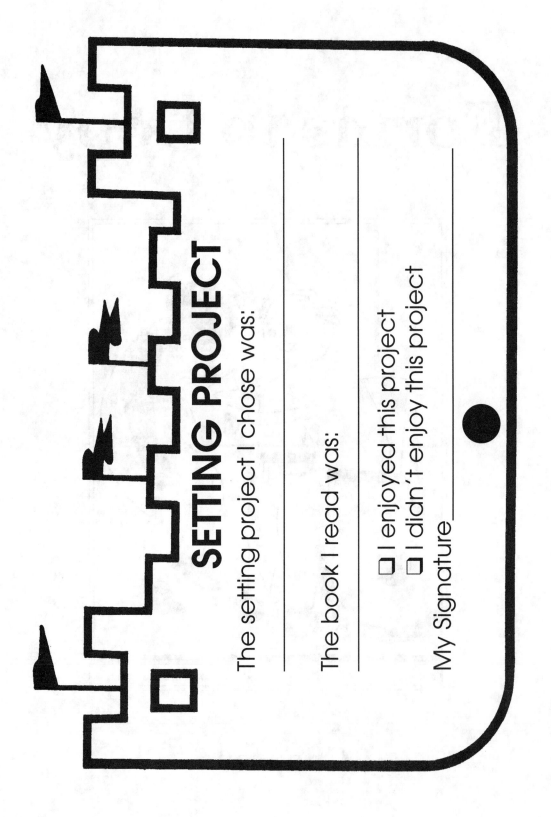

SETTING PROJECT

The setting project I chose was:

_____

_____

The book I read was:

_____

☐ I enjoyed this project
☐ I didn't enjoy this project

My Signature _____

Setting Wheel
Form 1.

Setting Wheel
Form 2.

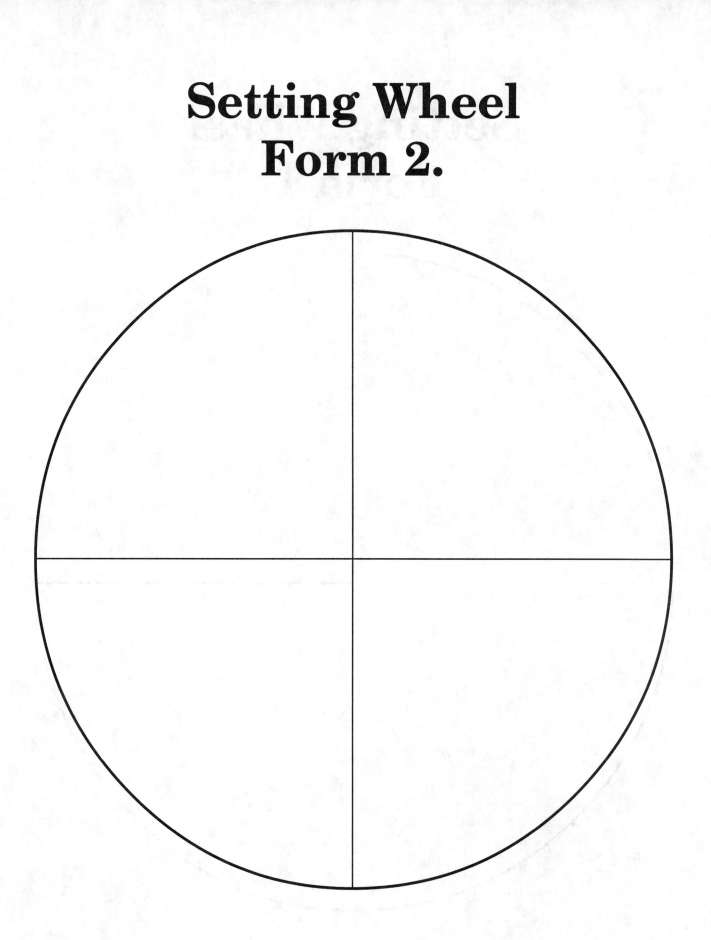

Let's Learn About Story Elements: Setting   Scholastic Professional Books

Book Chain Goal Sheet

Today's Date:

Name:

Number of books I want to read and include in my chain

_____.

Starting date _____   Goal ending date _____

Types of books (genres) I want to include:

- ❏ Adventure
- ❏ Biography
- ❏ Courage
  and Survival
- ❏ Fairytale

- ❏ Humor
- ❏ Historical Fiction
- ❏ Mystery
- ❏ Poetry
- ❏ Science Fiction

- ❏ Realistic Fiction
- ❏ Other:_____

Title: _____

Author: _____

Title: _____

Author: _____

Title: _____

Author: _____

Title: _____

Author: _____

Title: _____

Author: _____

ABOUT THE AUTHOR
Of...

BOOK-WRITE
BEYOND BOOK REPORTS
GREAT GRAPHIC ORGANIZERS
LET'S LEARN ABOUT STORY ELEMENTS: CHARACTER
LET'S LEARN ABOUT STORY ELEMENTS: PLOT

Michelle O'Brien-Palmer

Michelle received her undergraduate and graduate degrees from the University of Washington. Her career in educational curriculum development and design spans twenty years.

Michelle works with students and teachers in five to six different classrooms throughout the school year as she writes each of her books. Children and classroom teachers always play an integral role in the creation of her books and music.

- *Educational Workshops and Inservices*
- *School Assemblies and Workshops*
- *Educational Consultation*

MicNik Publications, Inc.
P.O. Box 3041
Kirkland, Washington 98083 • (425) 881-6476